W0006397

INTRODUCTION

Concise yet informative, *Spanish to go* is ideal for weekend visits to the beautiful country of Spain – a regular glance at the contents of this pocket-sized language book will ensure you'll never be lost for words.

Clear and precise, the pronunciation that follows each word and phrase has been devised to simplify the Spanish language for the English-speaking user, with the aim of producing more relaxed and flowing conversations with the people you meet.

Make the most of your Spanish adventure with *Spanish to go* – whether you're making a hotel reservation, finding your way to the beach or chatting up the locals, speaking Spanish has never been easier.

THE BASICS

Hello
Hola
oh'lah

Goodbye
Adios
ah-dee-os'

Good morning
Buenos días
boo-ay'nos dee'ahs

Good afternoon
Buenas tardes
boo-ay'nahs tar'days

Good evening
Buenas tardes
boo-ay'nahs tar'days

Good night
Buenas noches
*boo-ay'nahs
 no'chays*

Yes
Sí
see

No
No
no

Please
Por favor
por fah-vor'

Thank you
Gracias
grah'thee-ahs

You're welcome
De nada
day nah'dah

Thank you very much
Muchísimas gracias
*moo-chee'see-mahs
 grah'thee-ahs*

How are you?
Qué tal está?
kay tahl es-tah'

Fine. And you?
Bien. Y tú?
bee-en. ee too

Pleased to meet you (m./f.)
Encantado(a)
en-cahn-tah'do(dah)

Excuse me
Disculpe
dis-cool'pay

Sorry
Lo siento
lo see-ayn'toh

Pardon?
Perdón?
per-don'

Do you speak English?
Habla inglés?
ah'blah in-glays'

I don't understand
No entiendo
no en-tee-en'do

I'm English (m./f.)
Soy inglés / inglesa
*soy in-glays'/
in-glay'sah*

My name is...
Me llamo...
may lya'mo

Could you repeat that more slowly,
  please?
Por favor, repítamelo más despacio
*por fah'vor ray-pee'tah-may-lo mahs
  des-pah'thee-o*

Could I pass by?
Puedo pasar?
poo-ay'do pah-sar'

Why?
Por qué?
por kay

What?
Qué?
kay

Who?
Quién?
kee-en'

When?
Cuándo?
coo-ahn'do

How?
Cómo?
co'mo

How much / How many?
Cuánto / cuántos?
coo-ahn'to / coo-ahn'tahs

Where?
Dónde?
don'day

Which?
Cuál?
coo-ahl'

How far?
A qué distancia?
ah kay dis-tahn' thee-ah

Can I have...?
Me podría dar...?
may po-dree'ah dar

Can you tell me...?
Me podría decir...?
may po-dree'ah day-theer'

Can you help me?
Me podría ayudar?
may po-dree'ah ah-yoo-dar'

GETTING FROM A TO B

AIRPORTS & ARRIVALS

Where is / Where are the...?
Dónde está / Dónde están...?
don'day es-tah' / don'day es-tahn'

baggage reclaim
la recogida de equipaje
lah ray-co-hee'dah day ay-kee-pah'hay

luggage trolleys
los carritos
los car-ree'tos

help / information desk
el mostrador de información
el mos-trah-dor' day in-for-mah-thee-on'

ladies' / gents' toilets
el servicio de señoras / señores
*el ser-vee'thee-o day say-nyo'-rahs /
    say-nyo'res*

Are there any cash machines here?
Hay algún cajero por aquí?
ah'ee al-goon' cah-hay'ro por ah-kee'

Is there a bureau de change nearby?
Hay una oficina de cambio por aquí?
*ah'ee oon'ah o-fee-thee'nah day
cahm'bee-o por ah-kee'*

Is there a bus / train to the town centre?
**Hay autobuses / trenes que vayan al
centro?**
*ah'ee ah-oo-to-boo'ses / tray'nes kay
vah'yahn al then'tro*

TAXI!

Is there a taxi rank nearby?
Hay una parada de taxi por aquí?
*ah'ee oo'nah pah-rah'dah day tak'see
  por ah'kee*

How much will it cost to get to...?
Cuánto cuesta ir a...?
coo-ahn'to coo-es'tah eer ah

Take me to this address, please.
Lléveme a está dirección, por favor.
*lyay'vay-may ah es'tah dee-rec-thee-on',
  por fah-vor'*

CAR & BICYCLE HIRE

Where can I hire a car / a bicycle?
Dónde puedo alquilar un coche / una bicicleta?
don'day poo-ay'do al-kee-lar' oon co'chay / oo'nah bee-thee-clay'tah

I'd like to hire a car for a day / week.
Quisiera alquilar un coche por un día / una semana.
kee-see-ay'rah al-kee-lar' oon co'chay por oon dee'ah / oo'nah say-mah'nah

What is the daily / weekly rate?
Cuánto hay que pagar por día / semana?
coo-ahn'to ah'ee kay pah-gahr' por dee'ah / say-mah'nah

PUBLIC TRANSPORT

I'd like a single / return to...
**Un billete de ida / billete de ida y
 vuelta a...**
*oon beel-lye'tay day ee'dah / beel-lye'tay
day ee'dah e voo-el'tah ah*

What time does the next train / bus /
tram to...leave?
**A qué hora sale el siguiente tren /
 autobus / tranvía a...?**
*ah kay oh'rah sah'lay el see-gee-en'tay
 trayn / ah-oo-to-boos'/ tran-vee'ah ah*

Which platform do I need for a train to...?
**A qué andén debo de ir para coger
   el tren a...?**
*ah kay an-den' day'bo day eer pah'rah
   co-herr el trayn ah*

Which bus goes to...?
Qué autobus va a...?
kay ah-oo-to-boos' vah ah

Where should I catch the number...bus?
**Dónde tengo que coger el autobus
   número...?**
*don'day ten'go kay co-herr' el ah-oo-to-
   boos' noo'may-ro*

How much is the fare to...?
Cuánto cuesta a...?
coo-ahn'to coo-es'tah ah

What time is the last bus / train /
tram to...?
**A qué hora sale el último autobus /
tren / tranvía a...?**
*ah kay oh'rah sah'lay el ool'tee-mo ah-
oo-to-boos' / trayn / tran-vee'ah ah*

BY SEA

Where do I catch the ferry to...?
Dónde se coge el ferry para...?
don'day say co'hay el fay'ree pah'rah

When does the next ferry / hydrofoil
   leave for...?
**A qué hora sale el siguiente ferry /
   hidrofoil a...?**
*ah kay o'rah sah'lay el see-gee-en'tay
   fay'ree / ee-dro-foil' ah*

Possible responses

It's...   on the left / right
Está...   **a la izquierda / derecha**
es-tah'   *ah lah ith-kee-er'dah /
                           day-ray'chah*

straight ahead   over there
todo recto   **allí**
toh'do rec'to   *ah-lyee'*

Follow the signs above.
Siga los indicadores.
see'gah los in-dee-cah-do'rays

It'll cost...euros per day / per week.
Cuesta...euros por día / por semana.
*coo-es'tah...ay'oo-ros por dee'ah /
por say-mah'nah*

There's a train to...at...
Hay un tren a...a las...
ah'ee oon trayn ah...ah lahs

Your train will leave from platform number...
El tren sale del andén número...
el trayn sah'lay del an-den' noo'may-ro

You'll need bus number...for...
El número...va a...
el noo'may-ro...vah ah

The next boat for...will leave at...
El siguiente barco sale a las...
el see-gee-en'tay bar'co sah'lay ah lahs

BEDS & BREAKFAST

HOTELS & HOSTELS

Do you have any vacancies?
Les quedan habitaciones libres?
*lays kay'dahn ah-bee-tah-thee-o'ness
  lee'brays*

I would like...
Quisiera...
kee-see-ay'rah

I reserved a single room / double room...
**He reservado una habitación individual /
doble...**
*ay ray-ser-vah'do oo'nah ah-bee-tah-
thee-on' in-dee-vee-doo-ahl' / do'blay*

with twin beds
con dos camas
con dos cah'mahs

with a double bed
**con cama de
matrimonio**
*con cah'mah day
mah-tree-mo'nee-o*

with a shower and toilet
con aseo con ducha
con ah-say'oh con doo'chah

with a bath
con baño
con bahn'nyo

How much is...?
Cuánto cuesta...?
*coo-ahn'to
    coo-es'tah*

bed and breakfast...
alojamiento y desayuno...
ah-lo-hah-mee-en'to e des-ah-yoo'no

half-board...
media pensión...
may'dee-ah pen-see-on'

full-board...
pensión completa...
pen-see-on' com-play'tah

per night

por noche

por no'chay

per week

por semana

por say-mah'nah

I'd like to stay for...

Quisiera quedarme...

kee-see-ay'rah kay-dar'may

one night / two nights

una noche / dos noches

oo'nah no'chay / dos no'chays

a week / two weeks

una semana / dos semanas

oo'nah say-mah'nah / dos say-mah'nahs

Is there a reduction for children?
Hay descuento para niños?
ah'ee des-coo-en'to pah'rah nee'nyos

Do you have any cheaper rooms?
Hay habitaciones más baratas?
*ah'ee ah-bee-tah-thee-oh'nays mahs
  bah-rah'tahs*

Does the room have...?
Tiene la habitación...?
tee-en'ay lah ah-bee-tah-thee-on'

a radio / a television
una radio / una televisión
*oo'nah rah'dee-o / oo'nah tay-lay-vee-
  see-on'*

room service
servicio de habitaciones
ser-vee'thee-o day ah-bee-tah-thee-oh'nays

a mini-bar
mini bar
mini-bar

air-conditioning
aire acondicionado
ah'e-ray ah-con-dee-thee-o-nah'do

a hairdryer
secador de pelo
say-cah-dor' day pay'lo

Is there a night-porter on duty?
Hay un portero por las noches?
ah'ee oon por-tay'ro por lahs no'chays

Can I have a wake-up call at...?
Me pueden despertar a las...?
may poo-ay'den des-per-tar' ah lahs

I like to stay out late, so will I need a key?
Quisiera salir hasta tarde. Me hará falta una llave?
kee-see-ay'rah sah-leer' ahs'tah tar'day. may ah-rah' fal'tah oo'nah lyah'vay

I'd like breakfast in my room tomorrow.
Mañana quisiera desayunar en mi habitación.
mah-nyah'nah kee-see-ay'rah des-ah-yoo-nar' en me ah-bee-tah-thee-on'

What time is breakfast / dinner served?
A qué hora es el desayuno / la cena?
ah kay o'rah es el des-ah-yoo'no / lah thay'nah

The room is too cold / hot / dirty.
La habitación está muy fría / caliente / sucia.
lah ah-bee-tah-thee-on' es-tah' moo'e free'ah / cah-lee-en'tay / soo'thee-ah

Could I have some clean towels please?
Quisiera toallas limpias, por favor.
kee-see-ay'rah toh-ahl'lyas leem'pee-ahs, por fah-vor'

The shower doesn't work.
La ducha no funciona.
lah doo'chah no foon-thee-o'nah

I'm not satisfied. I'd like another room, please.
No estoy contento. Quiero otra habitación, por favor.
no es-toy' con-ten'to. kee-ay'ro o'trah ah-bee-tah-thee-on', por fah-vor'

Can you recommend any good...?
Puede recomendar buenos...?
poo-ay-day ray-co-men-dar' boo-ay'nos

bars
bares
bah'rays

restaurants
restaurantes
res-tah-oo-rahn'tays

night clubs
discotecas
dees-co-tay'cahs

Are there any areas I should avoid at night?

Hay zonas que debería evitar por la noche?

ah'ee tho'nas kay day-bay-ree'ah ay-vee-tar' por lah no'chay

I'd like to make a phone call.

Quisiera hacer una llamada telefónica.

kee-see-ay'rah ah-ther' oo'nah lyah-mah'dah tay-lay-fo'nee-cah.

Can I have the bill?

La factura, por favor.

lah fac-too'rah, por fah-vor'

CAMPING

Where is the nearest campsite?
Dónde está el camping más cercano?
don'day es-tah' el cam'ping mahs ther-cah'no

May we camp here?
Podemos acampar aquí?
po-day'mos ah-cam-pahr' ah-kee'

How much to stay here...?
Cuánto es...?
coo-ahn'to es

35

per day
por día
por dee'ah

per person
por persona
por per-soh'nah

per car
por coche
por co'chay

per tent
por tienda de campaña
*por tee-en'dah day
    cam-pah'nyah*

per caravan
por caravana
por cah-rah-vah'nah

Where are the toilets / the showers?
Dónde están los aseos / las duchas?
*don'day es-tahn' lohs ah-say'os /
    lahs doo-chahs*

Is there / are there...?
Hay...?
ah'ee

public telephones
teléfonos públicos
*tay-lay'fo-nos
poo'blee-cos*

local shops
tiendas
tee-en'dahs

a swimming pool
piscina
pis-thee'nah

an electricity supply
conexiones eléctricas
co-nek-see-o'nays ay-lec'tree-cahs

Where's the nearest beach?
Dónde está la playa más cercana?
don'day es-tah' lah plah'yah mahs ther-cah'nah

Possible responses

We have no vacancies at the moment.
Estamos completos.
es-tah'mos com-play'tos

I can recommend another hotel nearby.
Puedo recomendar otro hotel cercano.
*poo-ay'do ray-co-men-dar' o'tro o-tel'
 ther-cah'no*

How long do you want to stay?
Cuantos días se quiere quedar?
*coo-ahn'tos dee'ahs say kee-ay'ray
 kay-dar'*

It's half-price for children.
Los niños pagan la mitad.
lohs nee'nyos pah'gan lah mee-tahd'

There are no discounts for children.
No hay descuento para niños.
no ah'ee des-coo-en'to pah'rah nee'nyos

That'll be...euros.
Son...euros.
son...ay'oo-ros

MONEY, MONEY, MONEY

GETTING IT

Where's the nearest...?
Dónde está...?
don'day es-tah'

    bank
    el banco más cercano
    el bahn'co mahs ther-cah'no

currency exchange office
la oficina de cambio más cercana
*lah o-fee-thee'nah day cam'bee-o
mahs ther-cah'nah*

cash machine
el cajero automático más cercano
*el cah-hay'ro ah-oo-to-mah'tee-co
mahs ther-cah'no*

What's the current exchange rate?
Cuál es el cambio actual?
coo-al' es el cam'bee-o ac-too-ahl'

How much commission do you charge?
Cuánto es la comisión?
coo-ahn'to es lah co-mee-see-on'

I'd like to exchange these traveller's
  cheques / pounds for euros.
**Quisiera cambiar estos cheques de
  viaje / estas libras por euros.**
*kee-see-ay'rah cam-bee-ar' es'toss
  chay'kays day vee-ah'hay / es'tahs
  lee'brahs por ay'oo-ros*

SPENDING IT

How much is it?
Cuánto es?
coo-ahn'to es

Can I pay by credit card?
Puedo pagar con tarjeta de crédito?
*poo-ay'do pah-gar' con tar-hay'tah day
 cray'dee-to*

Do you accept traveller's cheques?
Cogen cheques de viaje?
co'hen chay'kays day vee-ah'hay

FOOD, GLORIOUS FOOD

EATING OUT

Waiter / Waitress!
Camarero / Camarera!
cah-mah-ray'ro / cah-mah-ray'rah

I'd like a table for one person /
  two people...
**Quisiera una mesa para una persona /
  dos personas...**
*kee-see-ay'rah oo'nah may'sah pah'rah
  oo'nah per-soh'nah / dos per-soh'nahs*

Could we have a table...?
Quisieramos una mesa...?
kee-see-ay'rah-mohs oo'nah may'sah

in the corner	by the window
en la esquina	**al lado de la ventana**
en lah es-kee'nah	*al lah'do day lah ven-tah'nah*

outside | in the smoking area
afuera | **en la zona de fumadores**
ah-foo-ay'rah | *en lah tho'nah day*
  | *foo-mah-do'res*

in the non-smoking area
en la zona de no fumadores
en lah tho'nah day no foo-mah-do'res

Could we see the drinks / food menu
   please?
Nos trae la carta de bebidas / comida,
   por favor?
nos trah'ay dar lah car'tah day bay-
   bee'dahs / co-mee'dah, por fah-vor'

I'd like to order some drinks, please.
Quisiera pedir unas bebidas, por favor.
kee-see-ay'rah pay-deer' oo'nahs bay-bee'dahs, por fah-vor'

I'd like...
Quisiera...
kee-see-ay'rah

a bottle of...
una botella de...
oo'nah bo-tel'lyah day

red wine
vino tinto
vee'no teen'to

white wine
vino blanco
vee'no blahn'co

sparkling mineral water
agua mineral con gas
ah'goo-ah mee-nay-rahl' con gahs

still mineral water
agua mineral sin gas
ah'goo-ah mee-nay-rahl' seen gahs

a glass / two glasses of lager*
una cerveza / dos cervezas
oo'nah ther-vay'thah / dos ther-vay'thahs
(*Mention brands to be more specific)

a glass of cider
una sidra
oo'nah see'drah

a glass of lemonade
una limonada
oo'nah lee-mo-nah'dah

a glass of cola
una cola
oo'nah co'lah

a glass of orange juice
un zumo de naranja
oon thoo'mo day nah-rahn'hah

a glass of apple juice
un zumo de manzana
oon thoo'mo day man-tha'nah

Do you have a children's menu?
Tiene un menú para niños?
tee-ay'-nay oon may-noo' pah'rah nee'nyos

I'm a vegetarian (m./f.). What do you recommend?
Soy vegetariano / vegetariana. Qué me recomienda?
so'ee vay-hay-tah-ree-ah'no / vay-hay-tah-ree-ah'nah. kay may ray-co-mee-en'dah

Does this dish contain nuts / wheat?
Lleva nueces / trigo?
lyay'vah noo-ay'thes / tree'go

I'd like to order...followed by...
Quisiera pedir...y detrás...
kee-see-ay'rah pay-deer'...e day-trahs'

Could I see the dessert menu?
La carta de postres, por favor?
lah car'tah day pos'trays, por fah-vor'

That was delicious. Thank you.
Estaba buenísimo. Gracias.
es-tah'bah boo-ay-nee'see-mo.
  grah'thee-ahs

Can we order some coffee, please?
Quisieramos café, por favor.
kee-see-ay'rah-mos cah-fay', por fah-vor'

Could we have the bill, please.
La cuenta, por favor.
lah coo-en'tah, por fah-vor'

There's been a mistake. I didn't order
that drink / meal.
**Se han equivocado. No he pedido esa
bebida / comida.**
*say ahn ay-kee-vo-cah'do. no ay pay-
dee'do ay'sah bay-bee'dah / co-mee'dah*

Is service included?
Está incluída la propina?
es-tah' in-cloo-ee'dah lah pro-pee'nah

Possible responses

May I take your order?
Le tomo nota?
lay to'mo no'tah

I'd recommend...
Le recomiendo...
lay ray-co-mee-en'do

Would you like...?
Le gustaría...?
lay goos-tah-ree'ah

Enjoy your meal!
Qué aproveche!
kay ah-pro-vay'chay

SIGHTS & SOUNDS

ATTRACTIONS & DIRECTIONS

Where is / Where are the...?
Dónde está / Dónde están...?
don'day es-tah' / don'day es-tahn'

How do I get to the...?
Como llego...?
co'mo lyay'go

airport
al aeropuerto
al ah-ay-ro-poo-err'to

art gallery
a la galería de arte
ah lah gah-lay-ree'ah day ar'tay

beach
a la playa
ah lah plah'yah

bus station
a la parada del autobus
ah lah pah-rah'dah del ah-oo-to-boos'

castle
al castillo
al cas-teel'lyo

cathedral
a la catedral
ah lah cah-tay-dral'

cinema
al cine
al thee'nay

harbour
al puerto
al poo-err'to

lake
al lago
al lah'go

museum
al museo
al moo-say'o

park
al parque
al par'kay

river
al río
al ree'o

stadium
al estadio
al es-tah'dee-o

theatre
al teatro
al tay-ah'tro

tourist information office
a la oficina de turismo
ah lah o-fee-thee'nah day too-rees'mo

town centre
al centro
al then'tro

train station
a la estación de tren
ah lah es-tah-thee-on' de trayn

zoo
al zoo
al tho

When does it open / close?
Cuándo abre / cierra?
coo-ahn'do ah'bray / thee-err'ah

Is there an entrance fee?
Hay que pagar entrada?
ah'ee kay pah-gar' en-trah'dah

Possible responses

Take the first / second / third turning
on the left / right.
**La primera / segunda / tercera a la
izquierda / derecha.**
*lah pree-may'rah / say-goon'dah /
ter-thay'rah ah lah ith-kee-er'dah /
day-ray'chah*

Go straight on.
Todo recto.
toh'do rec'to

Along the street / road / avenue.
Por esta calle / carretera / avenida.
por es'tah cahl'lyay / car-ray-tay'rah /
ah-vay-nee'dah

Around the corner.
A la vuelta de la esquina.
ah lah voo-el'tah day lah es-kee'nah

Over the bridge.
Cruzando el puente.
croo-than'do el poo-en'tay

It's a ten-minute walk down that road.
Está a unos diez minutos bajando esa calle.
es-tah' ah oo'nos dee-eth' me-noo'tos bah-hahn'do ay'sah cahl'lyay

SPEND, SPEND, SPEND

SHOPPING

Open
Abierto
ah-bee-er'to

Closed
Cerrado
ther-rah'do

Entrance
Entrada
en-trah'dah

Exit
Salida
sah-lee'dah

Where's the main shopping centre?
Dónde está el centro comercial más grande?
don'day es-tah' el then'tro co-mer-thee-ahl' mahs grahn'day

Where can I find a...?
Dónde puedo encontrar...?
don'day poo-ay'doh en'cont'rah

baker's
una panadería
oo'nah pah-nah-day-ree'ah

bank
un banco
oon bahn'co

bookshop
una librería
oo'nah lee-bray-ree'ah

butcher's
una carnicería
oo'nah car-nee-thay-ree'ah

chemist's
una farmacia
oo'nah far-mah'thee-ah

clothes shop
una tienda de ropa
oo'nah tee-en'dah day ro'pah

delicatessen
una tienda de exquisiteces
oo'nah tee-en'dah day ex-kee-see-tay'thes

department store
los grandes almacenes
lohs grahn'days al-mah-thay'nays

fishmonger's
una pescadería
oo'nah pes-cah-day-ree'ah

gift shop
una tienda de regalos
oo'nah tee-en'dah day ray-gah'lohs

greengrocer's
una frutería
oo'nah froo-tay-ree'ah

newsagent's
un kiosko
oon kee-ohs'co

post office
una oficina de correos
oo'nah o-fee-thee'nah day cor-ray'os

shoe shop
una zapatería
oo'nah thah-pah-tay-ree'ah

supermarket
un supermercado
oon soo-per-mer-cah'do

wine merchant
una tienda de vinos
oo'nah tee-en'dah day vee'nos

How much is it?
Cuánto es?
coo-ahn'to es

Excuse me, do you sell...?
Disculpe, tienen...?
dis-cool'pay tee-ay'nen

aspirin
aspirinas
ahs-pee-ree'nahs

camera films
carretes
cah-ray'tays

cigarettes
cigarrillos
thee-gar-reel'lyos

condoms
condones
con-do'nays

English newspapers
periódicos ingleses
pay-ree-o'dee-cos in-glay'says

postcards	stamps
postales	**sellos**
pos-tah'lays	*say'lyos*

street maps of the local area
mapas callejeros de la zona
*mah'pahs cal-lyay-hay'ros day lah
   tho'nah*

That's too expensive. Do you have
   anything cheaper?
**Es demasiado caro. Tiene algo más
   barato?**
*es day-mah-see-ah'do cah'ro. tee-ay'nay
   al'go mahs bah-rah'to*

I'll take one / two / three of those...
Deme uno / dos / tres...
day'may oo'noh / dos / trays

I'll take it.
Me lo llevo.
may loh lyay'vo

Where do I pay?
Dónde se paga?
don'day say pah'gah

Could I have a bag, please?
Me da una bolsa, por favor?
may dah oo'nah bol'sah, por fah-vor'

68

Possible responses

Can I help you?
Necesita ayuda?
*nay-thay-see'tah
ah-yoo'dah*

We don't sell...
No tenemos...
no tay-nay'mohs

You can pay over there.
Puede pagar allí.
poo-ay'day pah-gahr al-lyee'

That'll be...euros, please.
Son...euros, por favor.
son...ay'oo-ros, por fah-vor'

MEETING & GREETING

MAKING FRIENDS

Hi! My name is...
Hola! Me llamo...
oh-lah. may lyah-mo

Pleased to meet you. (m./f.)
Encantado(a)
en-cahn-tah'do(dah)

What's your name?
Cómo te llamas?
co'mo tay lyah'mahs

Where are you from?   I'm from England.
De dónde eres?   **Soy de Inglaterra.**
day don'day ay'rays   *soy day in-glah-*
                                        tay'rah

How are you doing?
Qué tal estás?
kay tahl es-tahs'

Fine, thanks. And you?
Bien, gracias. Y tú?
bee-en' grah'thee-ahs. ee too

What type of work do you do?
De qué trabajas?
day kay trah-bah'has

Would you like a drink?
Quieres tomar algo?
kee-ay'rays to-mahr' al'go

Two beers, please.
Dos cervezas, por favor.
dos ther-vay'thas, por fah-vor'

My friend is paying.
Paga mi amigo.
pah'gah me ah-mee'go

What's your friend's name? (m./f.)
Como se llama tu amigo(a)?
co'mo say lyah'mah too ah-mee'go(gah)

Are you single / married? (m./f.)
Estas soltero(a) / casado(a)?
es-tahs' sol-tay'ro(rah) / cah-sah'do(dah)

Are you waiting for someone?
Esperas a alguien?
es-pay'rahs ah ahl'gee-en

Do you want to dance?
Bailas?
bah'e-lahs

You're a great dancer!
Bailas muy bien!
bah'e-lahs moo'e bee-en'

Would you like to have dinner with me?
Quieres cenar conmigo.
kee-ay'rays thay-nar' con-mee'go

Can I have your phone number /
e-mail address?
Me puedes dar tu teléfono / e-mail?
*may poo-ay'days dar too tay-lay'fo-no /
e-mah'eel*

Here's my phone number. Call me some
time.
**Este es mi teléfono. Llámame cuando
puedas.**
*es'tay es me tay-lay'fo-no. lyah'mah-
may coo-ahn'do poo-ay'dahs*

Can I see you again tomorrow?
Quedamos de nuevo mañana?
*kay-dah'mos day noo-ay'vo mah-
nyah'nah*

Possible responses

I'd love to, thanks.
Me encantaría, gracias.
may en-cahn-tah-ree'ah, grah'thee-ahs

I have a boyfriend / girlfriend back home.
Tengo novio / novia.
tayn'go no'vee-o / no'vee-ah

Sorry, I'm with someone. (m./f.)
Lo siento, estoy acompañado(a).
lo see-en'to es-toy' ah-com-pah-nyah'do(dah)

I've had a great evening. I'll see you tomorrow.
Me lo he pasado muy bien esta noche. Nos vemos mañana.
may loh ay pah-sah'do moo'e bee-en' es'tah no'chay. nos vay'mos mah-nya'nah

Leave me alone.
Déjame en paz.
day'ha-may en path

Sorry, you're not my type
Lo siento, no eres mi tipo.
lo see-en'to, no ay'rays me tee'po

EMERGENCIES

Call the police
Llame a la policía.
lyah-may ah lah po-lee-thee'ah

My purse / wallet / bag / passport / car /
   mobile phone has been stolen.
**Me han robado mi monedero / cartera /
   bolso / pasaporte / coche / móvil.**
*may ahn ro-bah'do me mo-nay-day'ro /
   car-tay'rah / bol'so / pah-sah-por'tay /
   co'chay / mo'veel*

Stop thief!
Al ladrón!
al lah-drone'

Where is the police station?
Dónde está la comisaría?
don'day es-tah' lah co-mee-sah-ree'ah

Look out!
Cuidado!
coo-e-dah'do

Fire!
Fuego!
foo-ay'go

Where is the emergency exit?
Dónde está la salida de emergencia?
*don'day es-tah' lah sah-lee'dah day
 ay-mer-hen'thee-ah*

Where is the hospital?
Dónde está el hospital?
don'day es-tah' el os-pee-tahl'

I feel ill.
Me encuentro mal.
may en-coo-en'tro mahl

I'm going to be sick.
Voy a vomitar.
vo'ee ah vo-mee-tar'

I've a terrible headache.
Tengo un dolor de cabeza terrible.
*tayn'go oon do-lor' day cah-bay'thah
   tay-ree'blay*

It hurts here...[point].
Me duele aquí...
may doo-ay'lay ah-kee'

Please call for a doctor / ambulance
**Llame a un médico / una ambulancia,
por favor.**
*lyah'may ah oon may'dee-co / oo'nah
am-boo-lahn'thee-ah, por fah-vor'*

I'm taking this prescription medication.
Estoy tomando esta medicina.
*es-toy' to-mahn'do es'tah may-dee-
thee'nah*

I'm pregnant.
Estoy embarazada.
es-toy' em-bah-rah-thah'dah

Help!
Socorro!
so-cor-ro

I'm lost. Can you help me?
Me he perdido. Me puede ayudar?
may ay per-dee'do. may poo-ay'day ah-yoo-dar'

REFERENCE

NUMBERS

0 zero
cero
thay'ro

3 three
tres
trays

1 one
uno
oo'no

4 four
cuatro
coo-ah'tro

2 two
dos
dos

5 five
cinco
thin'co

6	six **seis** *say'ees*	**10**	ten **diez** *dee-eth'*
7	seven **siete** *see-ay'tay*	**11**	eleven **once** *on'thay*
8	eight **ocho** *o'cho*	**12**	twelve **doce** *do'thay*
9	nine **nueve** *noo-ay'vay*	**13**	thirteen **trece** *tray'thay*

14 fourteen
catorce
cah-tor'thay

15 fifteen
quince
keen'thay

16 sixteen
dieciseis
dee-eth-e-say'ees

17 seventeen
diecisiete
dee-eth-e-see-ay'tay

18 eighteen
dieciocho
dee-eth-e-o'cho

19 nineteen
diecinueve
dee-eth-e-noo-ay'vay

20 twenty
veinte
vayn'tay

21 twenty-one
veintiuno
vayn-tee-oo'no

22 twenty-two
veintidos
vayn'tee-dos

30 thirty
treinta
trayn'tah

31 thirty-one
treinta y uno
trayn'tah e oo'no

32 thirty-two
treinta y dos
trayn'tah e dos'

40 forty
cuarenta
coo-ah-ren'tah

41 forty-one
cuarenta y uno
*coo-ah-ren'tah
e oo'no*

42 forty-two
cuarenta y dos
*coo-ah-ren'tah
e dos*

50 fifty
cincuenta
thin-coo-en'tah

60 sixty
sesenta
say-sen'tah

70 seventy
setenta
say-ten'tah

80 eighty
ochenta
o-chayn'tah

90 ninety
noventa
no-ven'tah

100 one hundred
cien
thee-en'

101 one hundred
and one
cientouno
thee-en-to-oo'no

150 one hundred and
fifty
cientocincuenta
thee-en-to'thin-coo-en-tah

200 two hundred
doscientos
dos-thee-en'tos

1,000
one thousand
mil
meel

5,000
five thousand
cincomil
thin-co'meel

1,000,000
one million
un millón
oon mil-lyone'

DAYS OF THE WEEK

Monday
Lunes
loo'nays

Tuesday
Martes
mahr'tays

Wednesday
Miércoles
mee-err'co-les

Thursday
Jueves
hoo-ay'ves

Friday
Viernes
vee-err'nes

Saturday
Sábado
sah'bah-do

Sunday
Domingo
do-meen'go

REFERENCE

MONTHS OF THE YEAR

January
Enero
ay-nay'ro

February
Febrero
fay-bray'ro

March
Marzo
mahr'tho

April
Abril
ah-breel'

May
Mayo
mah'yo

June
Junio
hoo'nee-o

July
Julio
hoo'lee-o

August
Agosto
ah-gos'to

September
Septiembre
sep-tee-em'bray

October
Octubre
oc-too'bray

November
Noviembre
no-vee-em'bray

December
Diciembre
dee-thee-em'bray

TIMES OF DAY

today
hoy
oi

afternoon
tarde
tar'day

tomorrow
mañana
mah-nyah'nah

evening
tarde / noche
tar'day / no'chay

yesterday
ayer
ah-yerr'

now
ahora
ah-o'rah

morning
mañana
mah-nyah'nah

later
más tarde
mahs tar'day

TIME

Excuse me. What's the time?
Disculpe. Qué hora es?
dis-cool'pay. kay o'rah es

It's one o'clock.
La una.
lah oo'nah

It's quarter to eight.
Las ocho menos cuarto.
lahs o-cho may'nos coo-ar'to

It's half past two.
Las dos y media.
lahs dos e may'dee-ah

It's quarter past ten.
Las diez y cuarto.
lahs dee-eth' e coo-ar'to

Five past seven.
Las siete y cinco.
lahs see-ay'tay e thin'co

Ten past eleven.
Las once y diez.
lahs on'thay e dee-eth'

Ten to five.
Las cinco menos diez.
lahs thin'co may'nos dee-eth'

Twelve o'clock (noon / midnight).
Las doce del mediodía / de la noche.
*lahs do'thay del may-dee-o-dee'ah /
  day lah no'chay*

Now you can order other language, ACCESS ALL AREAS and
text-messaging books direct from Michael O'Mara Books Limited.
All at £1.99 each including postage (UK only).

ITALIAN TO GO	ISBN 1-85479-013-7
GERMAN TO GO	ISBN 1-85479-101-X
PORTUGUESE TO GO	ISBN 1-85479-066-8
FRENCH TO GO	ISBN 1-85479-084-6
BRITNEY SPEARS	ISBN 1-85479-790-5
CHRISTINA AGUILERA	ISBN 1-85479-780-8
CRAIG DAVID	ISBN 1-85479-948-7
EMINEM	ISBN 1-85479-793-X
S CLUB 7	ISBN 1-85479-936-3
BMX	ISBN 1-85479-145-1
HOOPZ	ISBN 1-85479-143-5
SK8	ISBN 1-85479-133-8
SNO	ISBN 1-85479-138-9
WAN2TLK? ltle bk of txt msgs	ISBN 1-85479-678-X
RUUP4IT? ltle bk of txt d8s	ISBN 1-85479-892-8
LUVTLK! ltle bk of luv txt	ISBN 1-85479-890-1
IH8U! ltle bk of txt abuse	ISBN 1-85479-832-4
URGr8! ltle bk of pwr txt	ISBN 1-85479-817-0
ltle bk of pics & tones	ISBN 1-85479-563-5
WIZTLK! ltle bk of txt spells	ISBN 1-85479-478-7
SEXTLK! ltle bk of sext!	ISBN 1-85479-487-6

All titles are available by post from:
Bookpost, PO Box 29, Douglas, Isle of Man IM99 1BQ
Telephone 01624-836000   Fax: 01624-837033
Internet: http://www.bookpost.co.uk   E-mail: bookshop@enterprise.net

Credit cards accepted.
Free postage and packing in the UK.
Overseas customers allow £1 per book (paperbacks) and £3 per book (hardbacks).